Compiled and edited by Natalie Vela
Illustrations by Agnes Lemaire
Color by Doug Calder

ISBN 13: 978-3-03730-161-6

Second edition

DISTRIBUTORS

USA
Activated Ministries
P.O. Box 462805
Escondido, CA 92046-2805
USA
Tel: 1-877-862-3228
E-mail: sales@actmin.org
www.activatedonline.com

Europe
Activated Europe
Bramingham Park Business Centre
Enterprise Way, Luton
LU3 4BU
United Kingdom
Tel: +44 (0) 845-838-1384
E-mail: orders@activatedeurope.com
www.activatedeurope.com

Canada
Coloring the World Productions
P.O. Box 1034
135 West Beaver Creek Rd
Richmond Hill, ON
L4B 4R9
Canada
E-mail: activatedcanada@ica.net

South Africa
Aurora Media
Suite 548
Private Bag X18
Lynnwood Ridge 0040
South Africa
Email: sales@auroramedia.org

Philippines
Activated Philippines
P.O. Box 1147
Antipolo City P.O.
1870 Antipolo City
Philippines
Tel: +63 2-985-2540
Email: activatedpi@activated.org

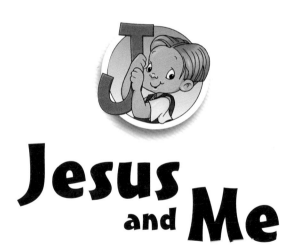

Jesus
and Me

Contents

Introduction

Hello, My little one!

My name is Jesus, and I love you very, very much! I came down to Earth and gave My life for you because I love you! Since you asked Me to come and live in your heart, I'm with you always. I will never leave you, and someday I'll take you home with Me to a beautiful place called Heaven!

2

In this book are some of My special words of love to you. There are little talks from Me to you, and all kinds of special things that I want to tell you. If you listen carefully, you can even hear Me whispering in your ear as you read these. Have fun! I love you!

Love, Jesus

I'm right there when you need Me!

It's so exciting to try new things! There are all kinds of things that can seem a little scary at first, like riding a tricycle, or going on a big slide or swing, or taking a ride in a big airplane, or learning to swim. If they seem a little scary to you, just shut your eyes for a minute, and ask Me to be right near you. And do you know what? I'll be right next to you, holding your hand or holding you on My lap. I'm always there to help you, because I love you!

6

Be a happy helper

There are all kinds of things you can do to be a happy helper and show My love to others! You can ask to help wash the dishes. You can put away your toys and books after playtime. You can make an extra effort to be neat and tidy at the table, and to eat all the food on your plate. You can obey right away. You can say "Yes, ma'am" or "Yes, sir" when you're asked to do something.

All of these are little ways to be a sample of My love, and doing them will help you grow up to be the loving person that I want you to be.

I'm your wake-up Friend!

When you wake up in the morning, just lie still for a few minutes and listen and you'll hear Me speak to you. I stay with you all through the night, and as soon as you wake up I like to talk to you, because you're so special to Me. You can talk to Me, too. Tell Me whatever you want and I'll listen very, very carefully.

You can ask Me to give you a happy day. You can ask Me to help you to be kind and loving with your friends. You can ask Me to help you to be a happy helper. You can ask Me to help keep you safe and careful when you play so that you don't hurt yourself. Then, once you ask Me these things, do what you can, and I'll do all the rest! I always hear your prayers, and I always answer you!—I promise!

I'm your wake-up Friend!

Then you can listen to Me and I'll tell you how much I love you. I can even tell you fun stories if you listen for long enough. I can tell you sweet things to tell your mommy and daddy or your teacher. If you have any questions, you can ask Me, and I'll answer you. I'm your fun wake-up friend, and I really like it when you talk to Me first thing each day.

I'm your wake-up Friend!

Bedtime promises

As you lie down to sleep,
just say a small prayer.
I'm waiting to hear it;
I'm always right there.
As you close your eyes
and drift off to sleep,
I'm there to hold you:
That's My promise I'll keep.

16

If you really want

a bedtime surprise,

I'll bring you sweet dreams;

we'll fly to the skies.

We can travel in spirit

to faraway stars!

We'll ride on the wind;

it's better than cars!

Bedtime promises **18**

From your real big Daddy

Are you ever sad when your mommy or daddy have to go away for a little while, and they have someone else take care of you and put you to bed? I know it's hard sometimes, and you miss your parents a lot. But thank you for being brave. And do you know what? Even if mommy or daddy have to go away for a little while, I never ever go away from you!

20

To My little birdies

You're My little birdie and I love to see you safe. I put you in your little nest and I give you all the food you need to grow—My Words that make you strong. Your mommy and daddy and brothers and sisters are all part of the little birdie family, too, and I watch over all of you!

I love to look down from Heaven and see you in your nest, playing happily with the other birdies. I have a great big smile on My face as I watch you care for each other and share your love and cheer.

Sunbeams of love

You are My little ray of sunshine. Every time you share your smile with someone, you're sending them a little sunbeam from Me. Every time you give a sweet hug or a friendly kiss, you're shining My love to that person. Each time you say, "Good morning," or "I love you," or "Thank you so much," you're being a little messenger of love from Me to those around you. So keep shining with My love! Be a little sunbeam for Me!

Did you know that when you send out My little rays of love, I love to beam them back to you? It's true! Try it sometime. If you give a cheery smile to someone, watch and see them smile back at you. If you speak words of kindness and love to others, see how they will answer back with kind words to you in return. If you give love, you will receive love.

We're best friends

What a special friend you are to Me. When I see that you're coming to spend time with Me, I give you My full attention. I love you very specially. I love to have you sit by Me and tell Me all your secrets, your thoughts, your dreams—everything about you. I love to listen, and I love to talk to you, too. We're the best of friends!

30

Making others happy

Sweet little birdie, thank you for sharing your love with those around you. Thank you for being kind and thinking of others. The more you think of others and try to make them happy, the more you make Me happy.—And the more I make you happy, too!

When you're afraid, just hold My hand

Lightning flashes big and bright! Thunder rumbles and rolls with a roar! If you feel a little frightened when that happens, don't worry! Everybody feels afraid sometimes. But when you do, just remember that I'm right next to you. I'm always near you. I'm never too far away to hear you when you call Me. If you're feeling a bit scared, ask your parents or someone who's nearby to pray with you. Or if you're all alone, you can just reach out and hold My hand and know that I'm right there with you, always. I'll be with you through every storm.

34

Build a tower of love

I like to be with you and watch you play sweetly with your friends. It makes Me very happy when you share and give. It makes Me very happy when you're kind and loving. It's like building a big, big tower out of building blocks. Every time you do something sweet, I give you one more block to add to your tower.

There are so many things that you can do to make your friends happy. You can share your favorite toys. You can let someone else have the biggest cookie for snack. You can give your friend a hug and pray for them if they get hurt. Every time you do something sweet and kind, it's like adding another block to your tower.

Build a tower of love

I have lots of blocks of many different colors—red, green, blue and yellow, and more—just like there are so many sweet things you can do each day. When you're kind to others, when you share, when you give, when you make someone else happy, I make you happy, too. Each block you add makes the tower bigger and higher and taller. When you give love, I bless you. I help you to be happy, and I help others to give to you, too!

Build a tower of love

40

Don't give up!

Are you learning something new and it's not so easy? Maybe you're learning to dress yourself, or put on your shoes, or you're learning to ride the tricycle. Keep trying!

Please don't be sad if it's hard at first. Sometimes you just have to keep on trying until you get it right.

Did you know that when a baby horse is born, it is very hard for it to stand up and walk? The little foal has to try and try and try again.

A foal who is learning to walk will try to get up, but then he'll fall back down because his legs aren't very strong. But he doesn't give up; he keeps trying and trying again. He falls down many times, but then he is finally able to stand on his little legs. He's a little wobbly at first, but in a few days he's able to walk and even run!

Don't give up!

So if you make a mistake, or if you're trying to learn something new that isn't easy, just keep trying. If you try hard enough, you'll succeed in the end. Just like the little foal is finally able to stand and walk because he doesn't give up, you'll be able to get it right. Ask Me to help you, and keep trying until you make it.

46

Don't give up!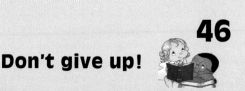

Your own special angel

Are you not feeling well? Do you have to stay in bed because you're sick? I'm sorry. But did you know that when you're sick, I send a special angel to your bed to help take care of you? Yours is here right now—by your pillow, or hovering above you, or sitting next to you, or standing on the floor by your bed. Your angel is here to help you get better. All the little kids who are sick and who pray, get their own angel of healing. I love you and I'm going to take good care of you.

Look before you leap!

Did you get hurt? I'm so sorry. If you come over here, I'll hold you in My arms and kiss away your hurt and make it feel all better. Did your mommy or daddy pray for you? If they did, then I've already begun to heal you and make your hurt all better. You can pray, too. I always hear your prayers!

50

Little bumps and scratches remind you that you need to go slower, or that you need to be more careful. Look around and pray before you jump off a rock or hop over something. It's important to look before you leap, or your shoe or clothes might catch on something, and you might take a tumble! It's a good lesson on going slow and being careful. But I'll heal you up quickly. Please remember to pray!

Look before you leap!

Count your blessings!

Have you ever really wanted something someone else had? Maybe one of your friends got something that you didn't get, like a nice new toy or a new dress, and you started to feel badly that you didn't have something like that. Has that ever happened to you?

Well, if you'll just stop for a few minutes and count the good things around you, you'll find that there are so many ways that I bless you, too.

54

You're special to Me!

Maybe someone else got a new toy, but maybe I will bless you with extra time with your mommy or daddy, or maybe you'll get to go somewhere or do something special. Your friend may be getting to do something really fun because it's their turn, but you'll get your turn later to do something special, too! I love each one of you dearly.

56

Playtime

Do you really enjoy your playtime? I sure did when I was a child. I used to run around with My friends and play games just like you do now. Sometimes some of us would fall down or get hurt—just like you do sometimes.

When you're playing, has it ever happened that you feel that something isn't fair, and you get upset and angry? It makes playtime no fun when there are bad feelings or arguments. What can you do about that?

58

Well, the best way to win is to be kind and loving. Even if you lose the game, if you've been loving, then *I* will call you a winner! Remember that the way I want you to play is by being nice to others and letting them have fun, too.

I like to have fun, too, and even though you can't see Me, I'm right there with you while you're playing. So think of Me playing with you, and how you would treat Me; and then treat others that way too. If you play that way you will always be a true winner!

You're important!

I'm the Good Shepherd, and you are My little sheep. You are such a cute lamb! I hear each one of My little sheep's calls. I hear it, and I come quickly and see what you need.

You can always call Me, and I'll come. I'm never too busy. When I hear you call Me, the most important thing to Me is to answer you! Did you know that? You're pretty important!

Do you feel very small, like you're just a tiny little person? Remember that I use tiny little things to do big things for Me!

I use the little honey bees to gather nectar and make the sweet honey that you enjoy eating.

I use the little raindrops to water the earth and all the flowers, and to fill the rivers for the fish.

I use little tiny seeds to grow into big trees.

I use little people—like you—to give lots of love and encouragement to others.

64

You're important!

When I ask you to give a little kiss and hug to someone, don't think it's a little thing—because I might use it to really cheer them up! Or if you help to wipe the table, or carry your dish to the kitchen, those are little jobs that are a big help.

I use your little smiles, your little hands, your little eyes, to be a sample of My love, and to show people how much I love them. So, My precious little one, you're very important to Me!

You're important!

Lights in the Sky

Isn't it a beautiful sunny day outside? Did you know that I made the beautiful sky and the sunshine for you? I wanted you to be able to run and play outside, and to enjoy My wonderful creation, so I put the sun in the sky, way up high. I made it shine down on you and give you light to see where you're going in the daytime—and to keep you warm too!

I also put the moon and all the stars in the sky so that they could glow and twinkle down at you, and watch over you while you're sleeping at night. The moon and the stars are a reminder that I love you, and that even when everything is dark, you can still see My light.

If you close your eyes and go to sleep, I'll make the night go quickly by. When you open your eyes, the sun will be peeking over the horizon, ready to bring you another happy day!

Sweet dreams

It's important to get rest and good sleep at night, because that's when you grow and become strong. Did you know that's when your body grows—while you sleep?

I give you dreams that you can enjoy and have fun in. Before you go to sleep at night, be sure to pray and ask Me to give you a good night's sleep and good dreams, and I will.

Did you know that when you sleep at night I speak to you and like to show you things in your dreams? Most of the time, when you wake up, you won't remember what I talked to you about, but be sure to think of Me as you go to sleep, and I will be there whispering in your heart!

Sweet dreams

Good night

I love you, My precious little child! Isn't it nice to have a cozy bed with nice pillows, bedtime stories, and mom or dad's goodnight hugs and kisses? All of these are gifts of My love to you. I have other gifts I give you when it's time to go to bed, too—secret gifts. Do you want to know what they are?

When you pray for a good sleep and good dreams, your special angel reaches into his or her pockets. Your angel pulls out little bottles filled with shiny, sparkly blessings, that look like little twinkles of light, and pours them gently on your head.

Good night

78

When you pray for your brothers and sisters and parents, your special angel pours sparkly twinkles all over them, too. When you pray for safety all through the night, your angel opens another little bottle and pours a beautiful stream of peace all over you. You can't see it, but if you close your eyes, I bet you can feel it!

All these are My special, secret, goodnight presents to you, because I love you so much. Sweet dreams!

FEED MY LAMBS

Bible verses for kids made fun

The *Feed My Lambs* series includes six colorful books with a total of 90 Bible verses on key Christian topics, simplified to make them easy for children to understand and learn. Each verse has a lively illustration that helps children relate the verse's meaning to their everyday lives.

As children become familiar with the Bible verses in the *Feed My Lambs* course, they will learn many important Christian truths and character-building principles that will stay with them throughout their lives. Try it today!

Feed My Lambs also doubles as a complete Scripture memorization course, and can help make this sometimes difficult task easy and enjoyable for children.

Kit includes: 6 books, guide for parents and teachers, 10 bookmarks, 90 stickers, 1 finger puppet, 2 award certificates, checklist, and audio CD.

Dimensions: 15 x 15 cm (6 x 6 inches)
ISBN-13: 978–3–03730–326–9

EARLY BIRD READERS PROGRAM

Learning to read made easy and fun!

The *Early Bird Readers* is a complete course designed to help young children learn basic sight-reading, and to have fun while they're doing it!

This series of 12 colorfully illustrated booklets provides a simple program that will help you give your child a head start towards the most important aspect of their basic education: reading.

The *Early Bird Readers* introduce over 100 words. Through the course of the readers, basic vocabulary is built upon one word at a time. Each word is repeated several times throughout the booklet in which it is newly introduced, as well as in subsequent books. Once the child has made their way through the booklets, they will have learned how to read a good deal of the most commonly used words in the English language.

Kit includes: 12 reader books, read along audio cd, flash cards, guide for parents and teachers, 2 bookmarks, 4 award certificates.

Get these and other great products for you and your children at your local Aurora distributor, or go to our website at www.auroraproduction.com.

Dimensions: 15 x 15 cm (6 x 6 inches)
ISBN-13: 978–3–03730–345–0